CITY PRA

Martin Wallace

Martin Wallace (signature)

Foreword by
The Bishop of Liverpool

The Canterbury Press
Norwich

First published 1994 by The Canterbury Press Norwich
(a publishing imprint of Hymns Ancient & Modern Limited,
a registered charity)
St Mary's Works, St Mary's Plain,
Norwich, Norfolk, NR3 3BH

Illustrations: pp. viii, 2, 22, 28, 40, 50, 60, 86 © Ray Price
pp. x, 12, 74, 96 © Caroline Wallace

British Library Cataloguing in Publication Data

A catalogue record for this book is available
from the British Library

ISBN 1-85311-099-X

*Typeset by Datix International Limited
Bungay, Suffolk and
Printed and bound in Great Britain by
Bell and Bain Ltd
Glasgow*

Foreword

by the Rt Revd David Sheppard, Bishop of Liverpool

Real prayer connects with real life experiences in very significant ways. I have discovered increasingly over many years the importance of personal prayer from deep in my own heart offered in the silent moments I try to make each day. In such time with God, the prayers we learn by heart or those that other people have put into writing for us also help us.

Prayer doesn't simply belong to the personal realm. In public worship we share concerns and open ourselves to our God corporately. It has long been a concern of mine that we often fail to connect these intercessions with the life of today's world in the same significant ways that might come naturally in the privacy of our own hearts. For the people of the city this is doubly hard because many of the traditional prayers which we have inherited were born in rural and very different settings.

Christians in the city need new 'urban images' which reflect God's ways with one another. Authentic prayer should be more than listing the news headlines and the sick list before God. It is right that we should pray for such specific people and places but there is also great value in the more poetic form of well written prayers from our place and our time.

I believe Martin Wallace's book offers a valuable resource to urban Christians, both stimulating our private prayer and enriching our shared prayers in ways that connect well with our experience of life in the City.

David Liverpool

Contents

CONTENTS

Preface

Every single one of these prayers is the result of actual observation and has been formed among growing city congregations.

The first forty five years of my life were spent exclusively in towns and cities: my first twenty two in London, Brighton, Southampton, London again, then Canterbury. The next three years were spent in Sheffield in a vast slum-clearance area among the (then) massive steel-mills. These were formative years when I had to conclude not only that our city-life often excluded God but also that our Christian imagery was too rustic in nature.

A further nineteen years in west and then east London convinced me that we had to work much harder at recognising that God was most certainly not absent in the cities, but that we were simply unaccustomed to seeing him there. I am very grateful to those Christians especially in Sheffield and East London who worked with me in developing an 'earthy' Christianity thoroughly grounded in the presence of God in the City.

It is my prayer that many, who either live or work in a city or large town environment, will find these prayers helpful in the daily round of their lives.

MARTIN WALLACE

Urban Images

At the beginning of the Bible we are taken into the Garden of Eden. In that garden, Adam and Eve disobeyed God, and in intimate imagery we are presented with a picture of God seeing what happened and then walking in the garden in the evening. He met with the couple and they discussed the situation together. The rest of the Bible is the steady progress from that ideal garden through various human cities on earth to the ideal city – the City of New Jerusalem, Heaven, in the book of Revelation.

My own earliest recollections tend to be pictorial images of the cities in which I have lived: sawdust on the floor of the butcher's shop, the view down the road from my window, the perspective along the school corridor. Later, as an older teenager, when I realised that Jesus loved me enough to die for me, that revelation came to me in the form of a picture – a vision – of the hand of Jesus pinned to the cross. Later, my call to full-time ministry was in the form of another mental picture

– a vision of God from his throne talking with me. Significant subsequent events have been similarly visual.

Pictorial presentations seem quite normal in scripture. Visions and dreams were part of life: Joseph dreamed of seven cows and ears of corn (Gen. 41), Isaiah saw a vision of God while in the temple (Is. 6. 1–13), Joel spoke of young and old seeing dreams and visions (Joel 2. 28–32), Peter had the vision of a sheet full of food (Acts 10. 9–16), and John's record of visions in the book of Revelation is quite stunning. Visual and enacted dramatic prophecy was the lifeblood of Hosea whose whole message was bound up with his marriage (Hosea 1. 1—3.5), and Jeremiah used very dramatic means breaking pottery (Jer. 19. 1–15) to make his point. With each of these, the visions or visual presentations were suggested by what was before them, and then used by God.

The parables of Jesus are all similarly drawn from visual observation, and his miracles were at the very least visually dramatic portrayals of God's love and power. His temptations in the wilderness sprung from reflections on what he saw – stone to turn to bread, a precipice from which to leap, and a panoramic view to claim as his own domain (Matt. 4. 1–11).

Elsewhere throughout the Bible we are presented with reflections on creation: the rainbow of Noah (Gen. 9. 12–17) is a sign of a new covenant and the psalms are full of references to the artistry of God and his skill in creating the clouds, valleys, animals, seasons, and so on (eg. Ps. 104).

But despite this very full visual and spiritual heritage, while there is much flowing today in terms of urban theology, urban evangelism, and urban community work, all of which is desperately needed, there is little on 'visual urban spirituality'. Yet without our roots fixed firmly in the spiritual depths of God today our evangelism, social care, and theology will wither and die. So what follows is not a book *about* praying in the city, but rather a book *of* prayers from within the city. Just as God walked with Adam in the garden of Eden, so he now walks with us in the streets of the city chatting about the events of the day and the images we see.

This collection is offered simply in the hope that it might encourage others to chat with God in the city, bouncing ideas together with him, between the truths of the Bible and the truths or urban life. Our task is to link the two in such a way that our souls are nourished and enabled to feed the urban mission into which we are called.

Adam said to God, 'I heard you in the garden.' (Gen. 3.10) Through all the noise of the city we need to recover that closeness with our creator. 'Lord, today we hear you in the city.'

M.W.

INVITATION

Come to me

I pass through the automatic doors
Of the supermarket.
It takes no effort on my part, Lord.
No pushing or pulling, no straining or heaving.
As I draw near – so they glide smoothly open.

'Come to me' you said.
'Draw near.'
Your arms are open like those doors,
And into your love I walk.
The gates of the city of heaven – New Jerusalem,
As described in your Word,
Are always open.
All I need do is draw near.
I do not have to convince you or impress you.
You call it grace.

Show me, Lord, the opportunities
To walk through all the open doors
Of grace
You place before me
Today.

Heavy-laden

Why is it Lord
That this bus,
Designed to transport adults,
Assumes we only need a tiny space
For our legs
As we sit,
With no space at all
For our heavy bags of shopping?
'These shopping trips will be the death of me!'
I overhear from the large overburdened woman
    behind.

You take me back to the story in the Bible
When the Israelites who carried the Ark of the
    Covenant
Containing the Ten Commandments on blocks of stone
Stumbled under its heavy weight
And a man called Uzzah steadied the Ark
And fell dead,
Overcome by the weight of the fear of the Lord
Through having touched that holy object.

Our secular lives are so easily stifled
By the compression and the weight of daily living.
Our spiritual lives are so easily stifled
By the compression and the weight of fearful hearts.
I hear you say gently and simply,
'Come unto me you who are heavy laden
And I will give you rest,
Even on the bus.'

Spiritual direction

We stand on the crossroads
At the heart of this community
Where shops and banks and travellers meet,
And buses and cars and lorries thunder by.
There are signs everywhere:
Shop names, advertising slogans, traffic signals.
But most striking of all
Outside the parish church
With its own sign and notice board
Is a post carrying two other signs
To a Sikh Gurdwara and a Muslim mosque.

Each notice claims to be equally valid.
The choice is startling and demanding.

And you said
'I am the Way.'

In the choices I have to make today, Lord,
Personal, physical, spiritual, emotional –
Help me to follow in your Way,
And in your Way
Only.

Getting the green light

The lights have suddenly turned green,
And the driver in front is taken by surprise
And stalls his engine.
From the side road
The other driver
Unaware his light had turned red,
Brakes ubruptly.

As we wait here in the middle of the traffic
This seems to be a picture of your relationship with
     me:
For when I become
Simon the Pharisee – bigoted and narrow in my
     horizons,
Herod the King – ruthless and opportunist in my
     decisions,
Mary the adulteress – caught in a web of moral failure,
You turn the light red and command that I stop.

And then with equal surprise,
When I become
Peter the disciple – ready to leave the familiar,
Paul the apostle – ready to change,
Mary the mother – ready to risk my reputation,
Those are the times
You turn the light green and command that I go.

I acknowledge that I am caught unaware so often
And what is more, I notice
You seem to prefer
The green light.

Entry into God

Each gate is different, Lord.
Wooden, iron,
New, old,
Painted bright and neatly latched,
Or broken, rusty and swinging loose.
Yet each one marks the entry point,
The boundary into the home of another.

And you, Lord, are the gate – the door.
So you said.
So it is as I come to you
I enter into your reality, truth, mystery,
    and into your home.
Never locked, easy to enter.
Not a barrier, not a flight of steps.
My desire to enter is all that is needed.

I know that as I cross each spiritual threshold
It is the same me.
But now I catch a glimpse of Heaven.
As I step cautiously in my mind
Over the boundary
Through the gate.

And as I walk down my road
By all these gates
My inner life
Is sustained.

Uniqueness

As you and I walk down this terraced street
Where all the houses seem to be from a common mould
And each door looks the same,
It would be easy to be mistaken
And assume that those inside each house
Are from a common mould.

You and I know, Lord,
That each household has a different story
Of happiness, heartache, and health,
   wealth, weariness, and worry,
   sadness, solitude, and sickness,
   energy, encouragement, and excitement.

I see pictures of biblical villages,
With square white houses all the same,
When the same assumption could be made.
Yet you cut through all of that
And treated everyone differently:
'Follow . . .'; 'Return . . .'; 'Give away . . .';
'Be reborn . . .'; 'Tell everyone . . .'; 'Keep silent . . .'.

Keep me alive, Lord,
To the special uniqueness
Behind each door.

Feeling at ease

I enter my local video store
For a wholesome family film,
But somehow the atmosphere
Feels dark and furtive,
With its association of blue movies
Kept under the counter
And violent horror stories
That line most walls.

I enter the betting-shop
Where everyone seems to know
What to do and where to go
To place a bet,
As all the customers
Laugh and joke together
Like old friends.

I enter the church
And I watch the new man
Who doesn't know
Where to sit,
Which book to use,
When to stand or kneel
Or who to ask.

Where do you feel most at ease, Lord?

STRUGGLE

Yearning for God

This is London
Where the signs all read
Labourers – no vacancies;
Job Centre – no vacancies;
Hostels – no vacancies;
Bed and Breakfast – no vacancies.

People's hearts also have no vacancies
For many here are full –
Full of sadness, anger, anxiety and weariness.
In this snack bar I see eyes
Staring blankly over lengthy cups of tea.
This is the city
Like Bethlehem – once
Yearning for help and direction and love:
Yearning for God to come in the flesh,
And make a difference.
Not a historical story of long ago.
Not statistics to be announced in the news,
But real people loved by you,
With crushed lives.

I have a feeling, Lord,
You've been here before.

Blessing through struggle

The bus arrives and the jostling begins
With those who have been sitting on the wall
Lurching forward to be ahead of the queue.
It is a struggle, Lord, not to be left on the pavement
Stranded with the push-chair
And the screaming, hungry child,
After the bus has left, full.

The scene here is a symbol of so much in the city:
The struggle to keep the children from crime;
The struggle to make the money last the week;
The struggle to find energy after a heavy day at work;
The struggle to keep the house decent;
The struggle to find quiet space in overcrowded rooms.
And especially,
The struggle to find
Space to be conscious of your presence:
Energy to live out your loving forgiveness.

Yet somehow your blessing is discovered in the
    struggle,
Just as Jacob wrestled and struggled with you.
And although he was left with a limp
Your deeper blessing never left him.

Lord, I pray for my friends and my neighbours
That they may know your blessing
In this struggle of living.

Identifying with the marginalised

The crowds picket the police station
With their chants and slogans and banners.
A regular scene in the city.
Like the Palm Sunday crowd who chanted
'Hosanna' when you rode into Jerusalem
And the Good Friday crowd – a different crowd? –
Who chanted 'Crucify'
And shouted for the life of Barabbas
When you were paraded before them.
Then it was outside the city
Making you the marginalised one
And the placard was fixed which read
'The king of the Jews'
In Hebrew, Greek, and Latin
Because you are the saviour of the whole world.

The city cannot understand
For its values are not your values,
And its ways are not your ways.
But if only they knew –
For
I suspect
That you might be among the aggrieved crowd
Outside the police station
Identifying now with those chanting
And feeling
Marginalised.

Hidden wealth

You lead me, Lord, around the back streets,
Behind the hospital and the market stalls,
Where people of all shapes and sizes
Who never emerge onto the main road,
Seem so extreme.
The grossly fat, the wheezy,
The thin and sunken and feeble,
The bandy, misshapen, who shuffle not walk –
Their faces portraying pain and struggle:
Poor diet, bad work, damp housing, ill-health.
Ironically, behind the hospital
Where health should be discovered.
It is a struggle simply to live.

You show me yourself in them, Lord.
You live in them to be loved – not patronised, or
    avoided.
They too are in your image
And you in theirs.
They show you to me much more than
A bejewelled cross set between silver candle sticks.

Yet this, Lord, is a major city of wealth,
Where outward wealth is paraded publicly
– a materialistic unreal wealth.
Somehow this hidden backstreet life
has a deeper significance:
A greater wealth
For here you are identified –
And revealed.

Lives transformed

These front gardens are tiny struggling pieces of
    ground
In terraced streets,
With walls and hedges
And insufficient light,
So the flowers and shrubs
Strain through the fog
To catch a glimpse
Of the sun.
And those that are able
Burst into bloom,
A riot of colour and shape
Visible all the way from the junction.

And in the homes
Behind these gardens
Are people who struggle
To catch a glimpse –
A sight of you.
And some have managed to catch that glimpse –
A sight of you,
And have been transformed
And have burst into bloom –
Into people whose lives
Reflect nothing less
Than your glory.

Clearance

Lord, look at the green grass
Growing through the cracked pavement.
See the windows all boarded up,
The chimneys lifeless and the doors unhinged,
The yards full of broken glass.
Where once there was a thriving community
Now there is a ghost town.
It has all gone:
The laughter of children
The sound of ball games
The gossip of the neighbours
And even the rows with the drunken husbands.
There is nothing but silence.
Yet the ground itself cries out for human life
As the ground cried out for the life of Abel
Mourning his passing.
His death was violent and unrequested,
As was the death of this community.

Here it was the result of a decision
To close the docks
Once vibrant with life.

Yet somehow Lord
I have a feeling
You stayed around.

PRAYER

Fragrant prayers

The chimneys belch forth their clouds of steam
And smoke and dust,
Polluting your world and my lungs,
Giving asthma to babies
And cutting short the lives of adults.
Their clouds rise and then fall on us
As from nowhere.

In your temple when sacrifices were offered,
The sweet-smelling fragrance
Was intended to rise and appease you
Through your nostrils.

In Heaven, we are told,
Clouds of fragrant incense rise
Carrying the prayers of the saints of earth,
And your response
Is to shower this planet
With love.

May my prayers
Be not
Polluting smoke
But a
Fragrant incense
Bringing a response
Of divine love.

Speak Lord

Lord, the phone booth in the street
Is quite different to my phone at home.
For at home I expect the phone to ring:
I have incoming as well as outgoing calls,
Whereas here, on the street corner,
I do not expect the phone to ring.

I feel that much of my life with you
Is represented by this booth:
Outgoing calls only to you.
Rarely aware you want to speak to me.

I can't stand here and pretend the phone will ring.
I can't manufacture your voice calling me.
I can only say to you
Here and now
Like the boy Samuel,
In the Bible,
When you want to call,
'Speak, Lord,
For your servant is listening.'

Prayerful obedience

Lord I saw the tower block fall flat today
From carefully placed demolition charges.
Flats built only thirty years ago.

I saw the great ball soaring through the air
On the end of a chain
Hurled by a crane
Casting down the Victorian terraces of homes.
The very ground shook.
You felt it too.

You felt it way back when
The walls of Jericho fell.
Then you showed your people
The power of prayerful obedience
Through the force of sound waves.

I wonder Lord
Have we lost a sense
Of prayer
And obedience
That results in the dramatic
Bringing down
Of walls and barriers?

Silent mystery

I sit in church, Lord,
Very aware of your presence,
Glad I can draw aside
From the hustle and bustle of the street.

Yet even in here
I can hear
The regular bleeping of the pedestrian crossing
    monitor,
The distinctive rattle of the diesel taxi engine,
The screech of brakes at the traffic lights.

Somehow I hear you telling me
Never to sever the relationship
Between the silence of mystery in worship
And the noise of everyday life,
For in the junction of the two
Is you
The Lord of Heaven and Earth.

Thank you

We take for granted
The refuse collectors and road sweepers,
The delivery of letters and of milk bottles,
The corner shop and the supermarket,
The street lights and telephone lines,
The seats and the bridges,
And you, Lord.

So I stop on this busy corner,
To do nothing more
Then simply take it in,
And say
A very heartfelt
'Thank you Lord!'

Lord of all

We wander through the market, you and I, Lord.
You seem at home in the bustle and the colour.
We pass the cheap blouses and shirts
And you call to mind your children in the Far East
Used as slave labour to machine these clothes.
We pass the cheap groceries and tea and coffee
And you call to mind your children in Africa and Asia
Unable to eat because we buy their cash-crops
   so selfishly.
We pass the tropical exotic fruit
And you call to mind those places and cultures
Where you are equally present.
We pass the cheap framed pictures
And you call to mind the variety of artistic ability
You freely give to all of your creatures.
We pass the cheap watches and bracelets and
   medallions
And you call to mind 'the lilies of the field
Who neither toil nor spin'
Yet are adorned beautifully by you.

Among all the noises
Your presence
And your thoughts
Come loud and clear,
Lord of the market.

SIN

Mind the gap

When the tube train draws in at the station
The loudspeaker urges
'Mind the gap! Mind the gap!'
And we all have a care
For the gap between the train and the platform.

I think today Lord that we have lost that care
Of the gap between heaven and earth
            between yourself and ourselves.
You are holy and we are sinful,
You are love and we are selfish,
You are good and we are deceitful,
You are pure and we are lost.

Yet we treat you with over-familiar contempt.
Restore, please Lord,
A sense of your majesty and grandeur
To us in our century
Of disrespect.

Or one day I fear
We shall fall down
The gap.

Hypocrisy

I walked through the market today, Lord,
And on the way
I thought I had some bargains
Of clothing and gifts.
But now I check the box
I find very shoddy goods,
Badly made,
Probably by poorly paid labourers.
I look back
And the trader has
Disappeared.

I am enraged!
Your prophet Amos roared,
'Overcharge, use false measures,
   tamper with the scales!'
I echo those words mentally
As I spot another trader
Selling not the polished apples from the front
But the hidden bruised fruit
   from the back of the display.

Yet who am I?
I thought I had victory over the trader.
Whereas, in fact, he simply had the victory over me.
What's the difference?
We become hypocrites so easily.
Lord, save us all!

Burning out the impure

From the six lane carriageway I can see
The council rubbish tip and borough incinerator.
There is a constant flow of yellow dust carts
And the smell of rotting garbage hits my nostrils.
I guess it must have been like that
In the valley of Hinnon
Outside the walls of Jerusalem
Where the children were sacrificed to the god Molech
Before the Israelites came and turned that valley into
The city rubbish tip.
Always burning, always pungent
To become a description of hell –
Gehenna –
Where the rubbish of peoples lives is burned
And those who do not want you
Are no more.

Lord, my journey past this site today
Asks me to take more seriously
The hidden forgotten doctrine
Of death and destruction
And fires of hell that consumes once and for all
All that is not pure and good and lovely
So that heaven may be holy
And fit for a king.

Reflection of heaven?

I see the overflowing sewer
Choked with debris and litter
And unmentionable garbage
From our effluent affluent society:
    Frothy, dark, pungent with flies, rats and disease.
I contrast it to Heaven which has
'The river of the water of life sparkling like crystal'
Flowing not from crumbling Victorian drains
But from the very throne of God,
And 'flowing down the middle of the city's street'.

I see the scant few trees
Vandalised by bored children,
Mutilated by powerful hands,
Used as toilets by loose dogs.
I contrast them to Heaven's 'Tree of life':
Full of leaves and full of life.
The heavenly leaves are
'For the healing of the nations'
Whereas the local ethnic groups
Feed on racism.
Culture, language, clothes, dialect, and music
All compete
Rather than co-operate
To complete the jigsaw
And complement the rainbow of human diversity
Which together
Reflects the glory of God.

Spiritual pointers

From the top of the multi-storey car park
I can see across the City.
Fingers of concrete reaching up to Heaven.
Office blocks, tower blocks.
All straining to be the tallest.
How different
To a few years ago,
When the skyline was made up of
Church spires,
Pointing with meticulously precise doctrine
To our destiny
With you in heaven.

Now the towers of mammon
And Babel
Cover our spiritual longing
And will be
Fingers pointing
To our destiny
Of destruction
Without you.

Giving of one's best

Lord, why do we have to put up with second-best?
Schools where parents can't fund the extra equipment.
Unemployment caused by those who live elsewhere.
Pollution from lorries serving the affluent suburbs.
A workforce that can find no alternative activity.
Officials gaining easy promotion,
    through lack of competition.
Broken appointments, low expectations,
    narrow horizons.
Buildings that have seen better days.
Overwhelming social issues
    crushing even the most able,
And constraints and constrictions that destroy the best.

You are not a God of second best.
You gave of yourself and you gave the best,
The best arena – the garden of Eden,
The best vision – through your prophets,
The best love – in Jesus your Son,
The best life – with the breath of your Spirit.

What a mismatch!
Lord, this is just not good enough
For those who live here,
Including you.

The weakest suffer

The little shops that cluster
On these backstreet corners
Are so convenient,
But very expensive,
And are slowly being forced to close
As people with transport
Drive to the supermarkets,
Leaving behind
The elderly with their shambling steps,
The mothers with their unwieldy buggies,
The poor with their lack of a car,
To use the ever-dwindling and restricted choice
Locally.

I hear you asking
Why Christians who claim to be born again
Insist on shopping at out-of-town supermarkets,
Thus forcing the weakest to suffer.

I do not hear you saying
That market forces
Are good or moral.

And I hear you, Lord,
Speaking to me.

Distorted image

You speak to me
Through that discarded hub-cap, Lord.
It is still silver
And reflects like a mirror,
But it distorts,
Enlarges,
Like a fish-eye lens.

My life is meant to be
An image of you
For those nearby:
A clear reflection.
And yet,
In fact,
It distorts,
Which is why so many
Have trouble
Seeing you
In me.

I do distort, Lord.
Yet in your love
You still condescend to use me
Rather than discard me,
Like this old hub-cap.

The stench of sin

Today it is so hot and muggy, Lord.
There is no wind
So all the heavy pollution of this city
Stays with us
Instead of being blown and dumped
On someone else.
I can taste the petrol in the air –
The leaded fumes of death that hover and kill.

Before you Lord I know that just as my car
Produces its life-threatening carbon monoxide,
So in my daily existence
I have created the heavy stench of sin
That sows the seeds of death in my own life
And in the life of others.

Even though you have saved me
I am still a polluting sinner,
Just as my now lead-free car
Is still not totally guiltless.

There is no way out
This side of the grave,
Which I help to bring quickly
On myself
And others
In the city.

INCARNATION

Meeting the outcast

I know you were in church with us tonight, Lord,
But I simply couldn't find you.
Oh – there were lots of people – comfortably full –
They all seemed very happy,
Singing, clapping, dancing.
Well-led from the front
With lots of songs and music
And a good message about
How we make people outcasts,
And how you were
An outcast.

So, after the service I went outside the church
Into the street
For a breath of fresh air,
And Tony came up from his house –
Divorced, unemployed, recent heart-attack,
On bail, named in the papers on trial for abuse,
On his way to the pub.
We talked for fifteen minutes
And we didn't mention you,
But there outside the church
I met you, Lord,
In the outcast.

He gave his only Son

These Christians tell me, Lord,
They will send their child
To a school out of this area
Because education there is 'better'
In a more affluent community.

They do not care that they are robbing their neighbour
And their school
Of their child
Who is a witness to the world
That you care for this place.
For they are only concerned
About the progress of the members
Of their own isolated family.

Lord, you so loved the world
That you gave your only child.

The release of one's child
To the local school
For the sake of this place
Is living the Gospel.

Actions speak so much louder
Than words, Lord.
Thank you for giving us your Son.

Human and divine

Outside the garage in the rain,
Along the gutter runs the water,
Covered with traces of oil and petrol
Forming a kaleidoscope of colourful pattern,
For the oil and water
Will not mix.

I reflect on your character, Lord.
I see you are human
For you ate, laughed, loved, cried, and slept.
I see you are divine
For you healed, walked on water, and rose from the
    dead.

The two sides of your nature
Are perfectly brought together
Like the genes of mother and father
In the creation of a new baby.
I am so glad
When I see your character
That I do not perceive oil and water,
But humanity and divinity
So intermingled
That you bring my humanity into your divinity
And your divinity into my humanity.

Present in the ordinary

In hospital I lay
Surrounded yet alone
Despondent, depressed, debilitated.
But you remind me that
I am 'fearfully and wonderfully made'
And you inhabit this creation of my body.
So you are here in hospital –
In me.

You point me through the words of another patient,
To the soap-holder on the wall:
To its symbol of hands washing
Looking like hands praying.
It is you who uses the ordinary
To remind me that you are very much present
Here
In the ordinary
If only we have eyes to see
And then
To pray.

Self-giving mediation

I sit in the traffic queue
Low in my car
Next to the huge wheel of a bus.
Large, round, black, rubber, tyre.
Without that tyre the journey will be impaired.
It is that, and that alone
Which connects the bus to the road

Connections are your business, Lord.
You sent Jesus
To connect earth to heaven
       humanity to divinity
       creature to creator
       death to life
       everyday life to spiritual truth.

As the journey proceeds
So that tyre is bruised, crushed, worn and punctured,
As was Jesus.
Connections involve such suffering and self-giving.
Mediation they call it.

Thoughts
From a bus tyre.

Present everywhere

From the theatres, galleries and shops
We cross the road and descend the steps
To the pedestrian underpass
Where they live
In cardboard shacks.
The homeless.
The under-class.

You seem to be everywhere here, Lord.
You are the prophet screaming at political leaders
That homelessness strips a society of dignity and value.

You are the priest declaring to pious congregations
That your mansion in heaven has many rooms.

But above all
You are the saviour
Who gave up your home in heaven
To be born into a feeding trough
And who in the faces around me here
Is very present.

Down from heaven

The notices shouting 'For Sale',
Are spreading down our street
Like a rampant weed engulfing us all.
Moving out, moving on, moving up!

Lord, you came from heaven down to earth:
Down, not up, the social ladder.
Why are Christians no different
   from the rest of society?
They follow so easily those others
Who want to move up to where there are
Wider streets and better schools.
I hear you beside me challenging that very hard.

You challenge too the accumulation
Of homes bought by property agencies
Who simply, as Isaiah said,
'Add house to house',
And then increase the rents, ignore the repairs,
Install noisy neighbours with dangerous dogs,
And refuse to discuss reviewing leases.

I recognise Lord, that
As a baby you chose a manger,
As an adult you chose to have nowhere to lay your
   head,
As a corpse you chose a borrowed grave.
From beginning to end
You identified
With the powerless
Who never move – Up.

Sustenance

She serves across the counter
Trading flour for cash,
In the shape of
Loaves of bread.
White, brown, wholemeal, sliced and uncut.
She reminds me of you, Jesus:
Born in Bethlehem, 'House of Bread',
Tempted in the desert to make stones into bread.
The Bread of Life yourself.
You offer yourself
To feed and sustain my soul,
So I can work for your glory
For 'my food is to do my Father's will'.
And in the broken bread
Placed in my open palm
As a reminder
Of your broken body,
Taken and eaten in remembrance
Of you,
We meet again.

And I thank you
For her
As she serves across the counter.

SALVATION

Seeing red

I stare across the kitchen table
At the vivid crimson of the ketchup bottle.
It reminds me, Lord, that
My 'Sins are red as scarlet',
According to your servant Isaiah.
Just as red screams 'danger' in the mind,
Or 'stop' at traffic lights,
Or 'help' as I cut my finger,
So my sins scream out to you:
The lies, the cheating, the selfishness,
The resentment and unforgiving thoughts.
My sheer rebellion against your love
Is violent red.

I know too of another red.
The red that flowed from his hands and his feet,
From his head and his side,
As Jesus hung on the cross:
That deep red blood that alone gives me life –
Eternal life.

Your son was given that I might live.
His red
Covers
My red.
You have spoken to me Lord
Of the important things of life
From a ketchup bottle.

Inner cleansing

An old mattress has been dumped
    at the end of my road,
Laying sodden and flea-ridden:
An eyesore for all.
Around the corner a mangled car seat
Is wedged dangerously high on the barbed wire
Above the broken wooden fence
Under the railway arch.
Further down,
Black bags of refuse make a pile ten yards long
Outside the row of shops.

The council's 'hot-line' is phoned
And this week it is all removed
Just for the asking.
We all feel lighter and brighter
As we walk to the bus stop today.

Lord, you have removed from my life
The rubbish and clutter
Just for the asking.

I keep creating more
But you constantly clean
The street of my memory and soul
And inside I feel lighter and brighter
As we walk to the bus stop today.

I will share this fact of grace
Today.

Building new Jerusalem

Metal poles
Vertical and horizontal,
Scaffolding.
The scaffold.
Execution.
Crucifixion.
Death.

Metal poles
Vertical and horizontal.
Scaffolding
Supporting planks
New building work
The creation of a new city.

In the scaffold of the cross
Lies the clue for the building
Of the heavenly city
New Jerusalem.

Lord,
You on the cross
Alone
Make that
Possible.

The eternal passover

The concrete flyover spans the roundabout below.
Thousands of wheels each hour.
It was built so that lorries may 'pass-over' local people.
These lorries come posing as angels of light and life
Bringing food and clothing and furniture
  we long to buy.
Yet in reality
They carry destructive junk-food:
Angels of death and darkness they are.
They pour out their carbon monoxide
Over us local people
As they pass-over.

This pass-over is totally ineffective
For these angels of death strike a double blow.

How unlike the eternal passover
You built in Jesus.
Who is the shield
Whose life and death creates the passover.
The angel of death can never touch us
If we place ourselves in your care.

I know the roundabout of life on which I now sit
Will one day spin me off
Into eternity and light and heaven
Because his passover
Is totally effective.

Real security

Across the tube I read his *Evening Standard.*
Economics dominate the headlines yet again:
Inflation, interest-rates, houses repossessed.
A few have more and a lot have less.
Unemployment, fear, benefits, failure.
We leave the station
And enter the tunnel of darkness
As do those with no money.
Into the unknown, the uncertainty.

What gives me security – deep security?
For all my Christian protestations, Lord,
About my soul finding rest in you,
I have more than a suspicion
That it is this material life
That makes me feel safe.
Why else do I enjoy the shopping malls so much?

Remove my possessions
And I come before you naked.
There is reality.
There is me.
And there is you.
My Lord
And
My God.

Here and now

The promise in Heaven is of light
From God
With no need of lamps
Or sunlight.
Whereas here I see a shadowy life
Of shady business deals,
Altered time-sheets,
Hidden child abuse,
Furtive stolen scenes of adulterous love,
Fearful of the light.

The City of Earth
Must become
The City of Heaven;
Must reflect
The City of Heaven;
For only then
Will we be free
As God intended.

I ask you Lord:
Will you bring it in with the end of time
Or are we to work at it now?
Is the Kingdom present or future?

And you reply –
'Both.'

Cared for and cleansed

A row of faces blankly sit
Staring at the small round screens
Of the launderette machines,
Watching their washing revolve,
Unaware that
Clothes are a sign from you,
A sign that you care.
For you made
The first clothes
For Adam and Eve
Who were expelled from Eden
But not from the presence of your love.
That was at the beginning, Lord.

At the end of the cycle
When the soiled clothes
Emerge clean and fresh and shining bright
You take me forward
To the end of time
When we will all stand
In robes of white
Clothed in victory and righteousness
Through Jesus.

REVELATION

All is revealed

Lord, I'm sure you see dear old Elsie
Sitting all day behind her curtains
Watching the world go by.
She thinks she is hidden
Behind the thick nets,
But all is revealed.

Long ago you tore a curtain from top to bottom
To reveal the Holy of Holies in the Temple
When your Son Jesus died.

Your apostle John on the island of Patmos
Saw you draw the curtain back
On the window of Heaven,
And witnessed what was indeed a Revelation.

Lord you are in the business
Of drawing back the curtains.
Please help Elsie to draw back the curtains
So she may be seen to be seen
And so be free to wave and smile –
To reveal and to be revealed.
For in that meeting
In that revelation
There may be
Holiness.

Continue learning

In our multi-cultural neighbourhood
The local comprehensive school
Is opting out for 'grant-maintained' status.
The fight is dramatic:
Staff, pupils, governors, local authority –
Locked in a combat involving colour, class,
    culture and creed.

Images of my schooldays rise up:
Very white, traditional – and detested!
Yet here and there
A friendly face
Emerges from my memory.
The teacher who laughed,
Inspired,
Even encouraged a vision of you, Lord.

You, who are my teacher,
Today you meet with me,
Your rebellious pupil.
The process now as never before
Embroiled in a cauldron
Of colour, class, culture and creed.

I am learning still Lord
As you see it all
And reach through it all
And use it all.
'Teach me my God and king in all things thee to see.'

Light in the world

We walk, you and I, Lord,
To work in the morning.
Past windows where the sun streams in
Giving light and brightness to each home
As the curtains are drawn back.
You remind me as we walk
That you are the Light of the World.
Lord, I long as never before for your Light
To stream through the windows of my soul,
So this morning I draw back my personal curtains.

And tonight, Lord, we return
Along the same street home from work.
Those windows that earlier received light from outside
Now reveal light from within.
Countless electric bulbs pour their brightness
Out into the street.
You remind me as we walk
That we, your disciples, are lights of the world.
Lord, I long for your Light to stream from my life
Through the window of my soul.

I am noticed

The pigeons wobble drunkenly,
Around my feet
Beneath the seat
In the small
But welcome
Park.
I sit quietly,
Unnoticed,
By commuters eating their sandwiches,
In their lunch break.
I shall never see these pigeons again.
I shall never see these people again.
I do not know their names
Or families
Or stories.
Yet I know, Lord, that you know them all.
You see even the smallest sparrow fall
(or the pigeon!)
And I recall that you added
That we are worth much more than the birds of
     the air.

And that reminds me, Lord,
That I too
am noticed.

Do not judge by appearances

From the outside
This house looks terrible:
Leaking gutter, fallen tiles,
Peeling paint on the door,
Broken hinges on the gate,
Sodden furniture in the garden.
And yet my breath is taken away
As I enter:
A fish-tank set in the wall in the hallway,
Sunken coloured lights in the ceiling,
A fully-equipped bar in the corner,
Mock-Tudor beams on the walls,
A huge television fixed in the alcove,
Carpet so thick it feels like grass,
And chairs designed for royalty.

You certainly meant it when you said
We were not to judge
By outside appearances.

What is true of his house, Lord,
Is certainly true
Of many of the people
I meet
In a day.

Spiritually anointed

The oily rag on the garage bench
Thrown aside by the young mechanic
Servicing my car
Takes me in different directions,
But always towards you, Lord –

The oil of the Spirit:
The oil to anoint the prophet or priest or king,
The oil to heal the sick,
The oil of the lamp for light to the world.
I long to be saturated with your oil
As is that rag.

Perhaps I am.
Perhaps like that rag I simply need to be wrung out
For the oil to appear more visibly
So that I may be more clearly
Healed and commissioned
And so more effective
In a healing and commissioning
Ministry.

The wind of God's spirit

As I stop at the garage
You, Lord, stop with me.
You talk as I fill my black radial tyres
With air
And remind me that your Word calls it 'Pneuma':
Air – breath – wind – spirit.
Pneumatic tyre filled with breath
So that my car can move
And be the vehicle it was intended to be.

You whisper that
When I experience the infilling of your Spirit,
Your 'pneuma',
It is not simply for my enjoyment.
It is so that I may become a vehicle
Able to move on in my faith, awareness, and service,
My communication of the Gospel.
Just as on the day of Pentecost
The wind of your Spirit
Enabled those early believers
To become
Vehicles of your Gospel.

Stopped in my tracks

Today a bomb exploded in the City
Killing some and maiming others.
Bereaving many, shocking all.

Lord draw near to everyone involved,
Including those who pressed the detonator.
Bring a just peace to Ireland.
This has been done to change the course of history.
Bombs do that.

There have been many times when similar tactics
Have been used on me:
Shocked, shaken, stopped in my tracks
By words, confrontation, illness or failure.
Bombs you have triggered in my life,
To make me stop and think,
Re-examine my direction and values and priorities.
In the end
Despite the pain
I am grateful to you.

But I am so sorry too
For all the grenades – emotionally charged –
That I have carelessly and thoughtlessly hurled
Hurting so many
Innocent people.

The corporate image

The sea of faces
Roaring down the pavement
In the January sales
Is like a tidal wave
Bursting upon the shore.
Hundreds and thousands,
All different
In shape and colour
In history and hope.
Yet each one in the image of God.

No one alone can be your full image, Lord.
But put together,
Assembled like a jigsaw
The human race
Corporately
Make up
The image of God.

In Oxford Street today
I saw
The image
Of God.

King of graffiti

The graffiti in the public toilet never changes.
Sometimes amusing, usually crude,
Sometimes awful.
At the bottom of the door it says
'Beware limbo dancers.'
More thoughtful lines include,
'Advertising stinks – most of us like the smell!'
'What colour is God?'
'History? Herstory? Whostory?'

Lord you left your share of graffiti.
At a feast in Babylon you wrote on a wall –
'Mene Mene Tekal Parsin.'
Quite unintelligible until your prophet Daniel
Interpreted your word to be judgement on the king.

When a woman was caught in adultery
Jesus scribbled words in the dust.
We don't know what he wrote
But it obviously made people think.

On that first Good Friday
The hastily scrawled words said,
'The king of the Jews.'
Mocking words that unwittingly spoke the truth.

You are King of graffiti too!

Awesome grandeur

Outside my window
The jet screamed overhead
And the mechanical diggers
Opened great chasms in the road
With the awful din of heavy engineering.
My attention is drawn by the noises
To both the heights of the sky
   and the depths of the earth.

You remind me that in the Old Testament
Your people with Moses
Had their attention drawn to your awesome grandeur
By the thunderous rumblings from Mount Sinai,
When both the sky above and the earth beneath
   shook violently.

'If I go to the heights of heaven you are there,
And if I descend to the world of the dead
   you are there.'
In the roar of the jet and the grinding of the digger
You speak to me of your grandeur
My Lord and my God.

TOGETHERNESS

Image makers

Look, Lord: our skyline is dominated by aerials.
See the forked wire for ITV and BBC
And for satellite TV the dishes –
Some white, some black.
(As well as the indoor aerials we cannot see).
We enter a house to discover
A TV in the lounge and one in the kitchen,
And one in each of the bedrooms.
Before each screen is a person – alone.

Yet when you made us
You said 'It is not good to be alone',
And you made a companion for Adam.

Lord, you are community.
You are Trinity – Three in One.
I understand it is as we reflect you in our life
And we conform to your image
That we find fulfilment.

To see these families
In separate rooms
Apart
Relating only to a pseudo-personal screen
Seems very unwholesome
Un-Trinitarian
Un-Godlike.
Lord, are we destroying your image in us?

Drinking with love

All in a day
I see in our street
A dog vomit on the pavement,
Children wipe noses on sleeves,
Men cough and spit in the gutter:
None of it a pretty sight.

At the end of the same day
I am in church
At a communion service
And as I am handed the cup
To finish drinking the wine
I see in it
From lips a thick film of grease
Laying on the surface,
Remnants of lipstick around the rim,
And lumps of spittle half-submerged
In what is a symbol
Of your life-giving blood.

I ask
'Lord, what would you have me do?'

And I drink it.

Real communion

You and I feel comfortable here, Lord
In the bar of our local.
I know you made and drank wine,
Enjoyed parties, made jokes and told stories.
Reminders of your past are all around me.
The woman in the corner who is paid for her favours
Yet comes to church
Is today's Mary Magdalene.
The electronic trivia quiz-machine
Asks questions and then infuriates
      by demanding answers
Like you who asked questions
And refused yourself to either give or be the answer
But simply the Way.
The pints are pulled and people drink
And return for more
Whereas you offered the Water of Life
That refreshes the inner thirst eternally.
The landlord shouts 'time'
As you said you will do one day
When the whole of creation will be rolled up
      like a carpet.

I am here in communion with you
            and with these people
            and with these stories of the gospels.
Sometimes, Lord, I can't help feeling
The communion rail in church
Should be more like a bar
Enabling communion like this.

Inter-relationship

The factory at the end of this road has closed,
So the shops locally lose their business.
The local schools give more free dinners.
'For Sale' signs abound.
Youngsters loiter aimlessly,
And the elderly are frightened to pass them,
Despite more police on the beat.
People eat less well,
So the doctor's surgery is full,
And everything is interconnected
Despite the fact that
Closing this factory
Was thought to be an isolated event
Taken by those
Whose homes
Are elsewhere.

Lord, in my bleaker moments
It feels as if society is being dismantled
Because people do not realise
That society is designed to reflect you
Who is Trinity –
Three Persons –
Interrelated and interdependent,
And every decision affects the rest.

Communication

Outside the Town Hall
You and I watch a group of aggrieved black men and
    women
Leafletting the white local councillors
Over alleged racism.
Black experience versus white perception.

To reach the Town Hall
They all need to cross the road
On a zebra crossing
Where black and white together
Make access to power
In the Town Hall
Possible.

Lord, you have said that in the City of Heaven
We find those of all races and tribes and languages
Bringing their differences
And jigsawing them together in worship
To make a whole.
I pray to you now with all my heart
That this confrontation
Will turn to communication
And a better city will emerge
So that others may see
A sign
Of the Kingdom
Of the City
Of God.

Longing for silence

You tell me that this City of Earth
Is to reflect your City of Heaven.
But reality is my neighbours:
When the parents work on night shift
Their children hold a noisy party
Until 6am Sunday morning.
The police call three times
And then give up.
Other neighbours
Shut their dog in the yard
All night
Barking loudly!
But not as loudly
As the couple who argue
At the top of their voices
All night long.
And then Lord
There is the crazy woman
Who walks the street in her nightie
Shouting at the world
While her neighbours
From their bedroom window
Pour on her their scorn
And the contents of their baby's potty.
And your Word tells me in Revelation,
'There was silence in Heaven for half an hour.'
Lord –
Take me now!

Known by name

We seem to be like sheep in the supermarket queue:
We may dress differently –
Baseball caps, turbans, flat caps, head scarves.
But we all stare blankly
Only reacting loudly
If a shopping trolley crushes our toes.
The woman at the check-out
Stares blankly
At the red and green light over which pass the
Macaroni, cornflakes, cake, and dog food,
Mesmerised by the computer's bell
Ringing with regular monotony.
We do not even speak as we exchange
Credit card for receipt.
Impersonal, self-absorbed,
Sweaty, money-grabbing,
Supermarkets,
We all use,
Showing
'We like sheep have gone astray.'
From the Good Shepherd
Who knows us all by name.

The good Samaritan

The streets here, Lord,
Are hot and dusty and airless.
They make me think of the road
    from Jerusalem to Jericho.
Here of course they are long and straight and boring,
Row upon row of Victorian terraces,
Unlike the twisting, cliff-edged road
To the Holy City.

That winding road had robbers
Waiting to jump out to steal and destroy.
We too have our rapists and muggers
Who dare people to walk alone at night.

As I walk by day
With eyes glazed and unfocused on the distance
Demons seem to jump out to steal and destroy faith
To question the purpose and reason for life.
'What's the point? I'm tired and exhausted.
Who cares? Not me.'

Then you send your modern equivalent
Of the Good Samaritan
Who draws near
Walks with me
Talks with me
And saves me for another day.

The personal touch

In the bank in the queue
We stand and stare silently at the publicity video
Encouraging us to take out a loan.
At the counter we stare through a glass panel
Push the bank-books into a metal drawer
And the clerk takes it on her side,
Stamps it and pushes it back,
Through the drawer,
Silently.
Human communication has ceased.
It is utterly impersonal.

Thank you Lord that you were born,
Laughed, cried, shouted, worked, ran, sat,
Healed, taught, touched, cared,
Bled, died, froze, and rose,
And still do today.

Lord, why can't my bank
Be more like you?

Counselling

You have accompanied me to the hairdresser, Lord,
And we watch the locks fall to the floor.
Years ago in Corinth
    Paul told the women in the church
To keep their hair covered.
Some say because hair displayed loose
Symbolised a loose woman.
Others say because in a newly mixed congregation
The men couldn't concentrate.
Either way, Lord, hair affected communion
Between you and between people.
Centuries earlier Samson had discovered
Exactly the same lesson.

In a strange way here too, Lord,
The hairdresser is a focus of communion.
Not necessarily with you
But certainly with the soul.
For souls are bared,
Opinions, experiences and feelings are shared.
The hairdresser is the acknowledged, untrained,
Social counsellor.
And in a mysterious way
Unknown to himself
He and his trade
Are doing something
Quite holy.

MISSION

Proclaiming the message

In this busy main road
The sign outside the church
Proclaims with irrelevant confidence
'A warm welcome awaits you
At the Women's Bright Hour,
And the Sunshine Club for children,
For God loves You!'

On the bench in front of the sign
Sit two unshaven men
In dirty coats and ill-fitting shoes,
Drinking their meths
From a shared milk-bottle,
With all their belongings
In the plastic carrier bag each guards so jealously,
Feeling neither welcomed nor loved.

Their simple existence
Denies the message
Of your church's sign.

Don't you sometimes despair, Lord?

God of the living

I know you wept Lord
When your friend Lazarus died.
You understand bereavement and grief
From experience.

Here in the cemetery
On Mothering Sunday
I am surrounded by hundreds
Who come to pay their respects,
And who long to meet again in some mysterious way
The loved mother who lives no longer.

I bring all these mourning people to you,
The living risen Lord,
And long that as on that first Easter Day
Your angels would appear
And say now as then,
'Why are you searching for the living
Among the dead?'

And you tell me, Lord
Your angels are simply
Messengers
And that
Is my role
Too.

Good news – bad news

We stand together, Lord, you and I,
Watching the rain trickle down the dirty window.
We see mothers cursing as they rush to collect
Their tiny children from the school gates,
Laden with shopping, umbrella forgotten.
We see drivers straining to see
Through mud-splattered windscreens.
Fearful of hitting
One of these mothers
For whom the rain is bad news.

But we also see the drains,
Cleared by the downpour for the first time in weeks,
And the trees
Drinking through shrivelled roots and parched leaves,
For whom the rain is good news.

Your Gospel is good news for the poor, outcast, and
      refugee,
And bad news for the rich, the secure and the
      powerful.
It is good news for the repentant and the seeker,
But bad news for the proud and dogmatic.

For me today, Lord,
Is your Gospel
Good News or Bad News
As we stand here watching
The rain?

Bringing release

These brick walls used to house
Victorian clerks so proud of their position –
Aspiring middle-classes:
These once bright red, yellow, and gleaming bricks,
Are now black and pitted and cracked
From a century of urban pollution.
Now they house an amazingly varied collection:
Teachers, welders, builders,
     nurses, unemployed and clerks.
All trapped
By mortgages, recession and interest-rates.
Standards of living decline
As they struggle and scream for release.

You take me back to Moses
And the oppressed Israelite slaves of Egypt.
Trapped by Pharaoh's greed for wealth:
'Create more bricks – from less material.'
The bricks were then a symbol oppression
As they struggled and screamed for release.

'I come to bring release to the captives'
Must be the echo
Of the Messianic Community today
As your church gets involved
In the real lives of its neighbours,
Trapped by these bricks.

Freedom from debt

You and I live together here, Lord,
In a community riddled with urban deprivation.
Unemployment, overcrowding, poor health,
Yet everywhere we are surrounded
By huge hoardings inviting us to spend
What we cannot afford.
Even the bank windows invite me to borrow
So I can spend
What is not mine.
Your prophet Jeremiah declared,
'Moneylenders oppress my people
And their creditors cheat them.'
I pick up a newspaper left on the bench
And you point to the adverts from the finance houses
Inviting me to phone them
    if the bank declines my request.

Lord, in my spiritual life you have paid the price of
    love
On the cross,
And even declared I have no debt to repay.
Help me to live my financial life
In a way that reflects that spiritual fact:
Free of debt.
Help me to help my neighbours
So that they too
Discover
That freedom.

Hear your call

Lord you gave new names to your friends:
Simon became 'Peter',
James and John became 'Sons of Thunder',
And Saul became 'Paul'.

I look around the pub tonight, Lord,
The little man alone in the corner is 'Zacchaeus',
The father by the bar who takes his son fishing is
    'Zebedee',
The woman flirting by the door is 'Mary',
The teenager from the tax-office is 'Matthew',
The political pundit is 'Simon the Zealot',
The heavily pregnant girl is 'Elizabeth'.

They are no different now to those you knew
Two thousand years ago:
A rich variety of people,
Unknowingly awaiting your call,
When the change they experience
Will be deeper even
Than a change of name.

May they hear your call
As we strike up conversation
Tonight.

The gamble of life

We tried to prevent it opening, Lord,
But failed.
Now the bored school-children, unemployed adults,
And the desperate and lonely
Gamble on these fruit machines
Doomed to lose.
Unable to resist the temptation.

Was a gamble at the heart of your creation?
Was it a gamble handing over the world to humanity?
Was it a gamble handing over your message to the
    prophets?
Was it a gamble handing over salvation from a cross?
Was it a gamble handing over your church
To Peter and his friends?
Birth is a gamble.
Friendship is a gamble.
Marriage is a gamble.
Faith is a gamble.
And beneath the cross
The soldiers gambled for the clothes of Jesus
Fulfilling a prophecy.
Gambling had a place in fulfilling your plan.

I will enter the arcade
To befriend those here
And gamble my chances
That you are with me.

Care for each one

I sit on the seat in the London square
Looking at the office block opposite.
Dismal, drab, and grey.
Dirty concrete with a flat face.
The windows all square in neat lines,
Horizontal and vertical.
Hundreds of people work within,
Faceless, nameless masses.

As I stare at that blank façade
I see a cross emerge.
The upright is a concrete beam between the rows of
    windows.
The horizontal is a concrete beam between the rows of
    windows.
That cross tells me
Even if those within do not know you,
Let alone love you,
You know and love and care about each of them.
You gave your life for them.
Each day they work
Within the reach of your cross
Without knowing it.

They will only know
And be transformed
If they are told.

'Whom shall I send?'
'Send me Lord.'

POSTSCRIPT

Postscript

If, having read these prayers and added your own 'Amen', you find that as you go about your daily life, the images here come to mind, and you begin to make your own connections between the world and God, then this little collection has been effective.

If you can go further and, as you walk down your street, wait for the lift, or fumble for change at the cash-till, find you begin to construct your own prayers of urban imagery, then we will have been effective together.

If you discover that your imagination has been fired, and you begin to share your prayers so that others begin to pray from within their own environment, then one authentic expression of urban spirituality will have taken root.